Barter

Barter

Poems by Ira Sadoff

UNIVERSITY OF ILLINOIS PRESS

URBANA AND CHICAGO

∞ This book is printed on acid-free paper.

Library of Congress Cataloging-in-Publication Data

Sadoff, Ira.

Barter : poems / by Ira Sadoff.

p.   cm.

ISBN 0-252-02834-1 (cloth : alk. paper)

ISBN 0-252-07120-4 (paper : alk. paper)

I. Title.

PS3569.A26B37   2003

811'.54—dc21   2002010966

ACKNOWLEDGMENTS

Earlier versions of some of these poems have appeared in the following magazines and anthologies:

The Agni Review: "Self-Portrait with Critic"
The American Poetry Review: "A Brief History of the Century," "An Uplifting Story," "Back Then," "In Siena," "Interim Report," "The Lethal Traumas," "Long Island," "Mahler," "Material," "In the Old Days," "The New Russia," "Scenario," "The Soul"
Best Poems of 2002, ed. Robert Creeley (New York: Scribner's, 2002): "Self-Portrait with Critic"
The Colorado Review: "Iran/Iraq"
Fence: "At the Creek Club," "The Cold War"
The Greeensboro Review: "I Forget Who Compared the Soul"
The Hampden-Sydney Review: "At the Frick"
The Kenyon Review: "Jazz," "What Kind of Man"
My Business Is Circumference, ed. Stephen Berg (Philadelphia: Paul Drey Books, 2001): "Did You Ever Get a Phone Call"
The New Bread Loaf Anthology of Contemporary Poetry, ed. Michael Collier and Stanley Plumly (Hanover, N.H.: University Press of New England, 2000): "Honeymoon in Florence"
The New Republic: "The Ex-Husband"
The Paris Review: "Like Angels," "Nature"
The Princeton University Library Chronicle: "Kindertotenlieder"
Webdelsol: "The Brightness"
The Yale Review: "Nefarious"

• • •

Thanks to Jane Mead, Claudia Rankine, and Laura-Gray Street for their valuable suggestions in helping me shape this book.

To Linda
and to Mickey Mizner and
the memory of her husband, John

But because truly being here is so much; because everything here
apparently needs us, the fleeting world, which in some strange way
keeps calling us. Us, the most fleeting of all.
Once for each thing. Just once; no more. And we too,
just once. And never again. But to have been
this once, completely, even if only once:
to have been at one with the earth, seems beyond undoing.

—RAINER MARIA RILKE, *The Duino Elegies*

CONTENTS

PART I

The Soul

The shaft of narrative peers down.
The soul's a petrified fleck of partridge this October.
Mud-spattered, it thinks it's brush, it thinks
it's one with the brush when God aims

just below its feathers. It's too late to raise the soul,
some ossified conceit we use to talk about deer
as if we were deer, to talk about the sun, as if the cold
autumn light mirrored our lover asleep in the tub.

Nevertheless, I want to talk about it. Those scarred bodies
on the hospital table, they're white chalk children use
to deface the sidewalk. The deer fed in the gazebo,
where the salt lick was barely safe from the fox.

And when the wind didn't drag my scent to her,
I sat listless, half-awake, and watched her hunger
surpass her timidity. I should have been changed.
I should have been startled into submission

by a very white light, I should have shed my misgivings
as her tongue made that sticky sound on the lick
and two startled animals stared into what St. Francis
called a mystery. I should bring her back, the woman too,

the woman who what why words fail me here.
I should sanctify the hospital gown as it slides down

the tunnel of the CAT scan, to see where
the nodules have spread into the thin, pliable tissues

we call the innards in animals, because they dwell
in scenery, they're setting for the poem, they provide
a respite from the subject who's been probed and lacerated,
who's been skinned and eaten away by the story

when I'm beguiled by the music the hooves made
on the pine floor. I can bring her back, can't I,
I'm bringing him back, the hero who was close enough
so I could watch what was inside his face hover and scatter.

Self-Portrait with Critic

One idiot took me for a Vietnam vet.
You have that tattooed damaged look.

Other descriptions? Jaded, pent-up,
wrathful, loyal, swerving toward hysteria.

Anyway, that's how she put me together.
She was a polyp in the clandestine tale

of what holes we are, what a factory
of piecework, stitched together

with bad wardrobes and bartered expressions.
To look at me, I hurt seems past tense,

synthesized into a gaze that drifts toward stable.
But passing is nobody's business, who you are

is a secret to everyone, that's American
as being an exception, believing in

your own invention, tinkering around
in a minor key since no one's listening.

And inside, let's not make it pretty,
let's save the off-rhyme and onomatopoeia

for the concert hall, let's go to the wormy place
where the problematic stirs inside his head,

something's jumbled inside the cells,
something chemical sticking to the walls

where the doctor looks down your throat,
down the tunnel where you sleep and wash up,

where you can't get over how dogs spar
with their masters, how Contras could tear

a newspaper in two and then bury the nuns.
Anyway, you can see how a sentence

might tear the heart out of someone,
closing in on and looking down at the mess

from some trim square of property
that's busily employed and invested

in making things work, with an ardor
and intensity that slips away into the ethereal,

all the while reciting some butchered version
of The Ancient Mariner, humming in your head

The *Pavanne for a Dead Princess,*
because you lean toward the luxurious,

the artful, the secondhand, once removed.

Did You Ever Get a Phone Call

Did you ever get a phone call from the past, pleading with you
to come back? As in a country song, Pain pulls up its dress, inviting you
to look. If it's not a husband and wife it's a Serbian hit squad,
the front of the bombed-out building so mangled and open, some widow's
cooking in her apartment while next door the bastard's undressing,
we can't see who it is, lying on the quilt in the bed you made together.

You know the voice, the exact pitch and inflection, the flap of it
from the window calling out. Is it yours? Can you stare at them like that,
at all those who've been vanquished, without recourse, the doggedly sad
who dream of satin instead of broadcloth? I mean of someone to love them
without inventing some self-portrait that looks like a war criminal
as he stands over the bodies with his hands behind his back.

Right now I'm sending this postcard from a resort town on the Isle of Wight.
Right now I've got my new wife going down to breakfast, humming.
Right now you can see why I turn away from the sink and its rusty drain.

But the news is like a warning in reverse, a collapsed barn
you remember with the cows still inside, incessantly mooing.
Little Sigmund Freud trying to climb back into the womb because he's sick,
there's no other explanation for that origin climbing,
for going back and repainting and replastering as if she were still in bed
begging you to bring her a magazine. I prefer the ruins
of another country: how quaint they are, where the Romans
once built a temple or two. I have friends who say, *I can't forgive the winter.*
Dear Gods, they say, *you wouldn't pilfer a shadow, would you?*

In the Old Days

Some days I lose track of my happiness,
plodding through the meadow thinking of something
grim I remember. It was a banal little town,

with cliques for the kids, wardrobes
fashioned by the Sunday *Times*. Everybody
who wrote poetry, I thought, came from that town.

Everything was tantamount, approximate,
a shovelful of dirt, a car rattling in the driveway,
loading my arms with packages, and as I emptied them

requiring I be adored. You know that bully
of a poet, that clumsy oaf certain powerless women embrace,
fucking the armor and the damage, waiting to be slapped?

Well, there was a sliver of Whitman on my knees
tending to the wounded, kissing their hands,
dying to hold one in my arms, to go on and on,

and leave them stammering by the window.
That was the old days. I forgot when I set fire
to ROTC files, when I sat in jail—for whatever sick,

ego-infested reason—to bring a sliver
of justice to Mississippi. More, I want to say
something of the hayloft above the sickly chicken coop,

and the turgid pea-sized pond out the window
squandered with ducks and duck droppings and a wire fence
electrified. There's no poetry in it. But we take the ladder up,

there's something infinite to the trip, something hand shaking,
there's the tremor I see in Matisse's cut-and-paste paper birds
all red and blue from some childhood I never had:

Linda in her white slacks and cream-colored blouse, infinite
the self-sustaining, replicating image of climbing up there,
losing an earring, it's nineteen ninety-two,

what we call the country's an incomprehensible babble
of shoves, litigation, strip searches, thefts of BMWs,
and out the hayloft door I see nothing but country, that nameless

scattershot splashing of hills and rumpled-up sugar maples,
and if my sexual obsessions stutter, linger, pause, accelerate,
if they can't be stitched together, if they're of no interest

to anyone, at least I am not alone, desperate, preaching
the parallel lessons of Dido and Aeneas.
Even if my ex-wife steals my every last Mozart sonata,

I can still smell the moldy straw, the weathered siding's
faded beige is a blessing to me, her body too, the story
she's telling me, my brain's on fire with it, years later, years

of happiness later, far from that dump we call governance.

Nature

In the old days there were characters
and settings: if you wrote snow
you could see wetness and whiteness
bending twigs of the cherry tree.

How many robins perched on that quince
in the snowstorm? Did the spill of milk
make us ill? And what did that say
about when the ladder fell? Everybody's sick

of naming a few familiar birds and trees
whose dilemmas are just like ours.
If we started out playful and restless,
flooded with all at once, we ended up

married to episodes. But don't give me
the Utopia of Childhood, the moody
little brats, what they extract,
how they suffer: I was a storehouse

of lassitude. I took everything personally,
I was a thumbnail sketch of the universe.
The branches are smarter than we are.
Their contract with stillness is limber

and listless. They bring us the sheen,
not of sparrows, not what we're thinking,
but juniper berries, just how green
they are soon after you clip them.

Interim Report

The schoolhouse closet was my favorite house of prayer.
Lately I've been paring down the pupil so light
can't enter it, the light that always meant the same thing
to Emily Dickinson. If you don't know the history of literature,
I'm leaving you at curbside. If you don't address God,

if you don't undress a close relative, if you can't
keep your accounts straight, I know a shelter
next to the Knitting Factory. There I saw
an old man knock for an hour, a skinny girl
with a star-shaped tattoo who demanded

immediate, authentic answers to the question,
What is the meaning of all this? I thought
her worry sugary, blurry, moonstruck, insufficient,
like the andante from a Mahler symphony
and other allusions meant to keep you knocking.

I left out myself, that November, and Jesus,
my teeth were chattering, and Mary, the myth
of you was what I'd been searching for.
Before this. Snow unprecedented. And the glare,
yes it could have been her face I turned away from.

Kindertotenlieder

In my head it's always the spontaneous trash
of the afternoon, sex and music,
shaving points, staving off the rent, gagging
on bad red wine, giving them your cash, getting a rise
out of how you made her gag. These are the great themes
of literature: sex as exchange value, deposit
and withdrawal, the investment part, sliding in and out
of each other in the service of wanting to obliterate
that bloody, brittle, severed-head sensation,
sleeping with someone you turn into material,
the raw material. In public, we say, *The term frontal nudity*
shall include pubic hair and the visible labia.
The sex is very good. The sex is terrible. Terrifying,
before and after. How could Mahler become a Catholic,
when meaning's beginning to accrue, insinuating itself, taking notes?
When he drives us to the passage on the lake
where his children drowned for no good reason—
there's a harp behind the strings,
the balmy composure of grief without the me in it,
not the hoarse and ragged voice of too much singing,
but where the dead spot has been urged to strip down
and dip into the water. In another language
swamp music is calling out its fiddle and accordion.
It's a cheap and tinny radio we listen to inside our heads.
There's the pleasure of being no one, of being satin,
the satin of her dress as you remember it, canceling the burdens,
the astonishing miscalculations, crossing out the crows

from the barnyard at dawn, the snapping turtles,
one on top of the other, the thick braid of the contralto's voice,
the pale blue fresco on the wall of the basilica
where angels appear, where the flurry of wings is so frenetic,
so rushed, so many pitches above the human ear,
you'd swear on your life they're perfectly still.

Mahler

Mahler endlessly repeats himself,
so one phrase, one symphony, et cetera, on a daily basis.
Can we still talk about Mahler?

So many tongues, surely one of them.
Cupping the water in his hands where
his drowned children in the pond are calling.

His wife in the hotel bed, touching
the other him. Let's just say sometimes
we have nowhere to turn. We wake up.

Wake again. In that same bed. Only the light
has moved. Some of us have sex for spite.
My theory is no one anymore listens to music.

Slid right off the table. Years are spent this way
recording, re-recording, stalling, imagining.
I wanted to tell you, in crude parallels,

about the future, how its texture
is a stutter, how we'll be snagged in the moment
where we know exactly who we are

and cannot change it. Was that my body
(so one phrase, one symphony, et cetera)
under hers again and again, suggesting

so many tongues, surely one of them
scores the same murky patter we sang,
we'll sing again. My theory is no one.

In the Jewish Mystical Tradition

In the Jewish mystical tradition, the body flying
is also the body falling. So to skimp or savor
just one person amounts to fortress and crypt, night sweats
for the minor characters. But if the body stirs

in several directions at once, if the human heaven's
more than a gasp and a shriek, we come back
to the stirrup, the nurse cupping her hands
for the all-at-once person, bloodied and self-absorbed.

That's the thrust of it, followed by washing your hands
several times a day to get the blank off, finding the spoon
veers away from the mouth, the door to her room's
slammed shut, the tongue making ala-ala-ala-ala sounds

in high-pitched shrieks as if houses had been razed
by bulldozers and lasers. You might bypass injunction,
impasse, you might call up the elixir of a person,
the hoarseness of her voice, brittle as enamel on the teapot.

The devotion's dumbfounding, shifting, forgetful,
philanthropic: a slip billowing up, a wheeze
in the surgeon's waiting room. Ideally
we like directness in a person: but what's to shelter us

from splintered and defective, infantile and helpless,
the want want want that wells up and scatters

in the place where we're broken, in the blank space
where the industry of everyone means nothing?

You can't raise a person like a subject, you can't erase her,
can't take her with you. You can't forget the body
shining. If not shining, raw and scrubbed clean.
Let someone else pray for a miracle, get on his knees,

be all briar and thorn: let them board the train,
stack the wood, powder the face, the face of all that stillness.

Like Angels

Like angels, we live many lives at once,
hovering over one with house plans, one unrequited,
another so quiet you have to turn the music up
so you can't hear yourself think. It's inevitable, then,

turning the corner someone hideous is likely,
someone bound to be unhappy, someone
whose fault you are. Someone wedded to the idea,
Once You Knew Me. Once, just possibly,

a chord was struck. I remember the top down:
it was breezy there, when sitting in your body was like
being glued to it. But I don't want to be accessible,
I don't want to read other people's minds,

don't want their tiny projection screens
pulled by ropes and pulleys, dropped into my bedroom
to illuminate the naked body as it squirms
with pain and pleasure. In the interim it's all titillate

and torment, stir and gyrate, sliding toward
a smudge on the sketchpad until
the aftermath meanders under the hotel window,
on the block that's nothing but a storefront

boarded up inside my head, where
I'm still married to the funeral's still inside me,

wearing black shoes and a silk tie,
rubbing me the wrong way, on a corner

where we could almost love the blankness
that's never mind to the avenue. We should recall
whose lips last touched the glass. Should, should, should.
Not what we whisper when we want her.

Fox Crossing a Field

I'm no St. Francis, I can't decide who the devil is,
who should live with whom, who should die happy.
Apprentice to the pasture, I linger like music—
on the enchanted, the marsh grass, the unascribed.

But in the meadow the first fox of spring—
correcting a sentence—has crossed over, spying
a killdeer, God's most stupid creature. When scared
she rolls over and spreads her wings. So spindly

are her legs she should be waddling at surf's edge,
not squawking in my birch grove. When I say
birch grove the light comes on: you can see in
the window: how calm the eye is. It's a monastery.

Nefarious

The literal poppies seem so paper-thin
that to be moved by them
is to be moved by a letter, a signature,

is to displace how red they are—
it's florid and rhapsodic to compare them
to late Beethoven sonatas, so obsessive

on so little material, a few clusters of notes
twisted and transfigured, darkened
and heightened before they're pulverized,

the memory of them more colorful
than the petals themselves, basically because
I can't finish a thought before words line up

and demand to be said: it's nefarious
to say *hotel room* and think *prison cell*
(the sink a foot from the bed), her scent before it,

looking out at the courtyard just before
the wrens break out into their high-pitched Eden,
before the lazy drawl of daily speech

darts up from the lobby. What's raw
about their unfettered sweetness, what's opaque
about the late night air, bleaching a tint at a time,

lumbers toward the scattered light
of morning until they're both hushed and dim.
I can't decide if I'm dense now or was dense then.

I hate to look down on them, striding
to their separate cars, looking sturdy and impatient,
making lists, meaning the poppies stand in

like "symbols of passion" in those medieval dramas
where secrets are borne by the body of Christ,
by the word of Christ. It's nefarious

to say *lumber* when you mean *dogwood*.
To forget the window and what's forged out there,
with duty and labor and contempt for the human soul.

Don't you get tired of talking to Jesus,
beseeching the not there, expressing sorrow
for all the sweaty, severed, transfigured spells

that slip through the soporific madness
of the moral lessons? How tempting it is
to compare them, to use a barrage of words

to drop over them. I wanted to write it down
as it appeared, with everything open about us:
not me, not the person jotting this down

from a distance, but how we watched them
approach the courtyard in their separate cars,
almost ready to take back the world—

I knew I was going back to the shattered
ordinary, the waking factory, the dimly lit abbeys,
the prosaic foot-tapping that pays for everything.

Whatever It Is

Whatever it is you call the freshness of dawn
it makes animals insane, clacking their beaks, barking
at a window pane (their breath a little cloud
that muddles and bewilders whatever work must be done).

There are buildings to raze, purposes, lists,
scores of humans to be devoured on the Killing Fields.
No wonder I'm drawn to cracked portions
of afternoons, drawing a blanket up to my neck at dusk.

You can read into it what you want:
blanched, colorless, doughy, sallow and pallid, yes,
they become inferences. Descriptive, but signaling too,
shutting down whatever's cracking open the door:

dozing on the desk, dreaming of a little illness
at the old folks home. Skateboarders streak past,
shouting them out of the way. That metallic sound
they make is like the ball in the roulette wheel.

Now they want to bitch about what they can
and cannot do, there's no civil liberties for them:
they can't smoke, they can't be promiscuous
enough to satisfy the whole neighborhood.

Maybe it *was* better when they played
cards together, when somebody else shuffled the deck,

when you could sit by the pool and leave tips
for the barboy, when in backrooms Ike knocked off Mike,

a little missile crisis, then sambas resumed in the ballroom.

.

The Lethal Traumas

Back there, yes back there, the bicycles
and the gauze over the camera lens, string music
in a minor key. I remember begins too many.

I forget too. Downtrodden, crestfallen,
the cynical voice in this poem crawls up my arm
with its clinical diction, its stacked-up metaphors:

the road, the train departing from the station,
the scorched-earth policy. If only I hadn't
come so close to the breathing, the not breathing.

The lethal traumas. The unbreathing parents
have vacated: now it's a friend sweating up his sheets
and thrashing. No one talks about politeness

at the foot of the bed, transcendence
and its mighty dispensation, the way the ditch
mounts its many meanings, its renewal policies

(asters growing over the if-onlys, it's been a good life
supplanting I want everything in the bed
with me, a complete inventory): the cyclical voice

in me wants to come back just as I am,
pulling up my pants, making adjustments,
wearing my mistakes like flammable tattoos,

the editing pencil check behind my ear
like a cheap cigar. I'm sitting by the pool, dreaming
of the dead man's float, suspended

between the only two visits to the hospital
that suggest the diamond speck in the bituminous,
the glass that shakes as he's drinking it.

Where We Lie Down in Heaven

Because it's a dry season, starlings
join the cedar waxwings
to peck the final cherries off the fruit tree.

Do we want to make something of it?
Do we want to push and shove
our way through the words, pay tribute?

When I think of been, I don't only think of green,
I think of the park where barking makes the grass shine.
That and the slick surface of the Arno. The river

where memories are so very cheap.
Cheapened by jewelry, leather bags and belts,
badly painted pictures, mass production, couples

whose daydreams are sparked by catalogs.
We're not short of subjects, opinions,
places to stay, ideas about why we cheat and lie,

vacation spots where we lie down
in heaven, shaded by frescos, olive trees,
banks of flowers. When the Ponte Vecchio

crumbled into the river, when pietàs
shattered along the bombed-out boulevards,
we may still be children, know nothing of repair

and piece together. I can't stand the earth
so parched we scratch at it with hoes and rakes
until I no longer know what it means to be a man.

Then I remember. Every few seconds
we want to sleep with someone new. We don't know
what to tamper with, how to excite the eye

so it won't settle on the shiny and available.

.

Long Island

I've spent the last few years with an eraser,
trying to uncover the masterpiece under the canvas,
scratching at the crusted-over surfaces:

were there windows? Certainly
there were gaping spaces and cherubim on bicycles
painted over with a dog and a few affairs.

The old subjects were the good subjects.
Love, greed, a stultifying awareness your arms
need replenishing. The paradise of shifting traumas

slivered into a chorus of bickering interior voices—
everyone had a defect, a mismatched seam, a flaw
you could see through, a pencil-thin crack in the cup.

So whatever was distinct about us,
bright or sensual, became a visit to the doctor
where the cancer's fastened to a rib, a series of periods

on an old piece of carbon paper. The twisted
machinations of childhood were nothing more
than a few coughs at the office, to be discounted later,

so while one was changing the channel,
another was soaking the dishes and the third
stood behind her, waiting to sexualize the moment.

Those who had maids understood slavery.
Those who had wives, bosses, those who decorated
according to magazines, those who sat in a chair

while a parent guided their pencil to the right answer,
the dead draped in flags, they also served.
While on the other side of town, on a more personal note

we didn't want to be no more nothing, so we slummed
at the chicken shack, where the dead flies on the counter
that looked like jewels were really roaches.

The Bangbus

The bangbus was battered and blazing.
Showing off, what unmuffled sounds we made.
In the late self-portraits of Rembrandt, there's too much green
and brown, as if he'd spent too many years
on his knees at the Dutch Traders National Bank.

It doesn't pay to have qualms, to apprehend, to cower
in the churchyard waiting for meaning
to color and solidify. Even if the paisley curtains shaded us
and helped us dream, dying was still inside:
turning suddenly onto the off-ramp, getting sideswiped,

or just changing lanes too quickly. On the bangbus
we chattered away: someone had finally discovered Kierkegaard
and wouldn't shut up as he twisted the cap off
a mighty fine wine. The headaches came later. I was so busy
becoming back then, it was like combing your hair

without a mirror: you didn't have to look
too closely about where to part, and who to part from.
And who can look at Giotto anymore
without thinking, *What was green like back then,*
and perspective? Didn't he start something

we forgot to finish? Riding the bangbus the excesses
were like peaches spilling out of bags of groceries.
On the bangbus I kept scraping the railing on the Hutch,

the world's most skittish parkway. It didn't matter.
I had sex there too, if we're talking metaphorically.

Whereas now I look at each thing closely
as I drive past it. The litter, how blowsy it is: tissue paper,
floating from one cloverleaf to the next. One lover
was a thief, the next needed Band-Aids.
You wanted to know who cut them up:

you could swerve and worry but you'd be curious:
how bad could it be, breaking down on the side of the road?

An Uplifting Story

It's so muggy out the person next door is clamming up
inside us. I say *we* because of cheap linguistic theory.
But I want to insert something personal, to get over
the rough spots, to get closer, to pan in, to take the long view,
to acquire professional assistance—these are other options.
Personally, if I hadn't left my ex-wife for the present tense,
I'd still be carrying mother with me and all her worries,
locked doors, the lies, sleeping in my nightshirt,
getting up to vacuum. Some wrong turns
argue for necessity. I'm not in love with the word spurious,
but there's no other way to get there. Ohio was happy
to be Ohio, where all the smiling faces in the windows
weren't mine. I was driving west, the way they do in literature
when crossing a frontier, my possessions were spilling out
of the back of the truck, so what could I do but turn around
and stop shouting at her—as if she'd been wrong for being her—
and look for signs: they were less towns than dots on a map
when you didn't have your glasses, so you had to guess
and settle on a position while sweating through your shirt
and trying to make nothing out of cornfield after cornfield.
I hated the thickness and the flatness, the stasis
of being yourself too long, being driven by a woman
you could hardly look at, no less see. The way it darkened
before my eyes, fireflies and frogs and rubber tires
in the burning fields, I thought how certain tribes set fire
to their furniture once a year, just to get my mind off it.
But now, for Midwesterners, a more uplifting story.

A few years later I was looking out from a camp
on Frenchman's Bay, and another woman, another way
of looking at it, was cooking something, something else
I'd never thought to ask for.

In the Emerald Isle

Skydivers curl and wisp: they forget
how human we are. How can they scrape the beach

without dying of fear? It's like riding my bike downhill
a hundred miles an hour into the lush rain-drenched valley

where they land on their rainbow-tinted parachutes.
My wheels are saucers: they buoy me up

so I'm flying too. While at home I scour pans
at the Patchogue diner. Depressing how scratched up we are.

After we're no longer angry sad titillated fiery run-down,
after we're tired of turning the ocean

into the bathetic infinity of the unsaturated self,
whatever's been sullied, whatever skin's been scarred,

whatever's dropped down and indented us,
we want it hammered out, we want a meadow, trifles,

the bromidic humdrum of a mall, someone beside us
in bed providing the sense of an ending,

even a false ending.

PART 2

A Brief History of the Century

Personally I can't figure out the scale of things.
Several years of misery follow me like a camera:
like a slug, I need to attach myself to something.

I'm stacking cans in a supermarket, reading Sartre
in a corner of the basement, adjacent to
picture windows and cardboard-thin developments.

The surge of miracles slow down just before
they get to our house: of course I hate my mother,
trust no one, school's a parish where the orphan

eats his porridge and scribbles frenetically on a pad.
An analyst might want to hear about it.
Drifting off, he might wonder,

Why would we set fire to Southeast Asia?
if he didn't take everything so personally. To this day
if I see Kissinger on TV, you don't want to hear about it.

You want to raise the silver bell to see what dish will be inside it,
the scent of it steams so close it's almost strafing,
but we're huddled outside the restaurant reading the menu,

everything looks good in advance till they take your job away.
It's nineteen seventy-five and Nixon's let the maniacs
out of the hospital, the explosive battering force of poetry

has not yet been debriefed: I mean it's years
before I'm standing on the corner like Whitman
and not like Whitman, on the corner of Fifth Avenue

and Fiftieth Street, where Alfred Knopf used to be,
waving a piece of paper in your face,
raising expectations so the horses in Central Park

are no longer glue—they clop down the path
to the pond where women under parasols are rowboats
in the sunlight before the century turns on them.

What Kind of Man

What kind of man hides in the duck blinds?
The days of description are over.
The days of It was April so Everyone Felt Hopeful,
where you could find in the swaying willow

a precise match for your own foggy sentiments.
She tightened her grip on the hospital bed,
because giving up meant subscribing to heaven
when the earth seemed all thistle and pod,

and digging up the flower beds. Don't hunt down
a pattern here. Don't think the man
at the bus stop wielding a crowbar stands for
a shiver when the sun disappears at four o'clock.

I'm not obliquely building a parallel, making a case.
I won't put sepia around it, walking the black labs
in the reeds while the quail fans its wings
like a deck of cards. I'd want Mozart there, Wolfgang

with the hysterical cackle of the child genius.
To see how he'd perform among the amorphous,
inchoate, obscure scores of the century,
when surprises are loading shells into cartridges,

when what I thought was starlight was chipped porcelain,
where John caught cancer, where Julie read me

her favorite story, where by accident suggested fortuitous
and calamity, where Pakistan set fire to India

or vice versa. What kind of man hides in the duck blinds
all afternoon, talking to himself, making animal sounds?

In Siena

There's a replica of Him writhing on the cross
they cart across the square, and what's the meaning there,
crossing your path? It's years ago, black and white tiles

in center city, where yesterday and today mean less
than coughs in a handkerchief. You can circumscribe
the fortress that saved them from the Florentines,

or didn't save them, I forget so much even as I try
to paint who's with me. I don't want her there,
I want the replica, where the hysteria's all theater:

there's an act or two followed by applause, a stroll
through a churchyard, an orchard, a sweet bloody glass
of Dolcetto D'Alba. . . . Now I try to retain the closeness,

keeping it vivid but not letting it overwhelm,
sticking with it, letting it shake me, going back to
she was available when I drifted toward her,

then it's so late, I still don't know where I'm going,
where to turn my attention next, what to lean on, going back
to the flash point, twisting it, granting its full weight.

Or else I could be sensible, make it smaller,
give it perspective, let daily life stake out its erasures
at the same time it heaps on the new. Then

where do the voices go, the seconds, the sex parts,
the window into someone else's life, the window wide open
for hours at a time, the breeze going through it,

you going through it, you going through
with that person what no one's been through,
before they have to . . . what's on their list of things to do?

Drive around the neighborhood, pointing to
the church you attended as a child, the bed where your child slept,
the kitchen table where you discuss the mortgage:

can you afford this pleasure, and what's the cost of looking?
What if you can't find the house you want,
all those hours expended? Then there's the paint

chipping off like small change, the door off its hinge,
the ugly stain where the tub once overflowed.
How urgent is it? To repair or let things decay as they are?

To Him, no question of a choice: it meant
loving everyone, taking on their suffering as yours,
shaving in their mirror, saving every scrap of paper.

The story's so familiar you're almost married to it,
you go shopping with it, you argue over who, yes who
could have possibly . . . when the blistering heat of that afternoon

suddenly flushes your cheek, and the person beside you asks,
What's wrong? You hardly hear them as their voice
wheels around the heart chamber, mingling, flooding to a stop.

Jazz

The slippery elms were statuesque,
one nice way of saying Ohio was a slag heap.
Most were stumps by the time I got there.

The War was going on, what we called The War.
In July the humidity was dense as a fortress.
Nights we swam naked in the quarry,

naked and paranoid. Next door, they were happy
in their Quonset huts: there were hunting dogs
to howl through the night, and there was scotch

if you needed it. I never found Pleasant Street,
but if you strolled around my block at dusk,
threads of inchworms would brush your cheek

from the remaining trees. You might hear
shouts and whispers from our tiny rented house.
So young we were, we left the windows open.

Really Ohio was just fine. With my friends
I played tapes of Bird and Diz in their toasty den
and reminisced about the great cooks of Chinatown.

When I left, they found fault with me
I guess. They never said. So please forgive me,
Ohio, my early misery: I'm still looking

to extract some essence, a surge, an eddy,
from that jittery splinter of a person
jazz spoke to: but I can't fill in the unbuttoning,

the abrupt, jagged melodies, the guttural likenesses.
Even in disease I found the elms heroic:
to have once towered over everyone in green.

Back Then

I couldn't understand the sonic boom,
the sacred texts of Vishnu might as well have been
        my mother's scribbled shopping list—
my favorite swami waved handkerchiefs above a colored vase
        and doves appeared. My father never knew
I drove around in Studebakers, listening to my friends
        grind down his gears, stomping on cigarettes
even as I recited Wordsworth's "The World Is Too Much
        with Us." In other words I thought the poet
a lawyer, representing some crime where I'm the victim:
        I got paid for feeling bad in three-four time.
I'd never seen that statue of Donatello's, the one that radiated,
        girl-boy, boy-girl. Heard the shapely mass
Mingus made of "Fables of Faubus," dreaming from his bass.
        I never listened to voices in my head
that made a screech of pure cacophony. Such as *The bride
        was battered by the bantam rooster.*
That mother never found herself another husband drove me
        fast and far away. Only a few of us
have premonitions. For the rest, even if we never hear the cough
        that's precursor to the cancer, we still expect
a handrail to hold, a house in the country, we don't expect the Wall
        to fall, to be dumber than dirt, for corpses to slide
ditchward in the rainstorm. Frankly we expect the fascist to stay
        a fascist, we expect the moral of the story.

At the Frick

I'll never understand how shimmer
and sailboat can slip out of the same sentence.
I'll never come close to Brancusi,

how surfaces shatter with all that apotheosis.
The gardener digs up shrubs, transplants
magnolias we know will die next season.

Metaphorically speaking, there's a seaside town
with spinster, missed opportunities
bobbing before her in the harbor, she's a good match

for my compulsive perfection-mongering,
squirming when a wrong note's played on the piano,
when my son won't pay attention to the museum

where I saw my first painting by Turner.
That yellow's with me still: late autumn—
that pale, that kind of fire—far from the clamor.

I learned the word print there, meaning
artifact, imitation, meaning sameness,
sameness of light. Like a bee stirring up the churches

I waited for the Savior there. But whatever
the gold medallion painted Madonnas signified
back then, there's wilderness between us.

To be luminous, it's the job of the boy soprano.
I was such a boy irretrievable in my happiness
and sullen too, that's what I most remember.

At the Creek Club

The caramel hills, the chockablock houses,
symmetrical patches of greenery awash with trees,
the eye clicking, spoke-like: you'd think
I was Cézanne, you'd think I was the only one.

A four wood, madam? Perhaps an iron would suit you.
By the time I got onto the course, there was nothing left
but duffers, and I dutifully followed them
through the swamps and ponds, out to the highway

and under the trees, where shame was two ducks
fucking, one beak thrashing the neck of the other.
Lamont Johnson, who sucked young men's cocks
whether they liked it or not, was out with me,

rifling their purses as they swung hopelessly away.
All the hours they took meant nothing compared
not just to his mouth but the shack where he took us:
charred cinder block and a couch whose cushions

had been eaten by a dog, a Formica cocktail table
with a shag rug of orange and brown, and a bathroom,
well, even my eyes wouldn't take me there.
I didn't live where I could be touched

in this tract after tract of a town: I was ethereal,
college bound, a budding genius, dazed, before and after.

The "I" so unstable it's all pinpricks and calipers,
a little probe of identity with quick-strike capability—

I can't even figure out where I lived, somewhere
between the Cuban missile crisis and the branch office
where those scantily clad secretaries wriggle and scream
before their bosses shoot buckets at the driving range.

We were nothing but a spot on the carpet, a spilled cup
of coffee you'd have to sponge clean. I finished wiping the clubs
with the rag I kept in my pocket, spotted with green.
Go ahead and make something of it, light a match to it: 1968.

The Cold War

The Russians lied because they couldn't be trusted.
Whereas we were always defending, but from a distance,
so culpable and palpable could be separated into whites

and less delicate fabrics. While their women
were bloated, dressed in babushkas and overcoats,
American adultery was take me out for a spin;

in Europe the mistress was stowed away
in a paid-for apartment, complete with utilities. So ennui,
fantasy, greeting cards with rhymed apologies,

makes me rethink scantily clad and blood-spattered Kansas.
A little spot of nothing, I was the instrument
of their accidents, but I'm not talking about me anymore.

Onerous, the spongy feeling you're not important. Too much
mainstream meandered near us, jumbling scopic
and phobic. I have no desire to get personal, to go back there

and accuse it, attach myself to the sensitive parts,
watching the clichés accrue like stock options: Kruschev
smashing his shoe on the table, side by side, an episode of Lucy,

Desi behind the set drinking away the profits,
afterwards adjusting his underpants, while in Russia, Russia's
just another person who doesn't know what she wants,

so when no one's looking she stuffs it in her pockets.

The New Russia

Now in Moscow they have opinions:
they like Janet Jackson, they don't like the Hansons,
there's no more thought police, no endless lines for the doctor.
They pine for purple silk and Pizza Hut, they like Mafia movies
where money's laundered, they like limousines,

everyone's off the dole, there is no dole
for the ten-year-old prostitutes. Even at twenty-two I knew
money's not important, that's Gatsby's mistake, so when I'm scrubbing
and mopping at the laundromat, taking home the purifying stench
of Clorox, I try not to worry I'll never be Oscar Wilde,

I'll never understand the mysterious business of Henry James,
I'll never have a cellar full of sixty-one Bordeaux,
the word Chateau might as well be scimitar, sacerdotal, chanterelle.
I'll never be Proust, the French romance with slumming
escapes me, my neighborhood's filled with duplicate Verlaines

and Baudelaires, the mentally ill eating out of garbage cans.
I'll never understand Robert Lowell's mammoth depressions,
a deferred annuity, the tragic love affair of Giselle,
and I hate the sinkhole where you look up at everyone
like a distant relative waving from the bottom of a well.

I'm only vaguely acquainted with the catastrophic,
my character's so banal I'm trafficking
in need, that's how American I am, for me an hour

is by the hour, my standards are vulgar, coarse—
character as honor, refusing a base impulse, is beyond me,

so when Mr. Lynch, formerly of the Exeter Academy,
walks in to dry-clean a few of his three-piece suits
I take one for myself (*Sorry, it never came back*).
I know abstractly we're all one, so welcome to our country,
Mother Russia, mother of my mother and father,

of the long metaphysical argument over the czar,
over whatever that clear, licorice, gasoline flavor liquor was.
In my new wardrobe I can debate fate and coincidence,
I can let the furies subside, the character me, I can wait
till Moscow's dreary as Rotterdam, the shipping lanes

brimming with cargo, longshoremen stuffing their pockets
with cartons of penicillin. So don't take it back, patriots
and transcendentalists: I still need a sweater, a demeanor,
a record player, a bookcase. I've got a few more happy months
coming to me, dreaming of my night at the Copacabana.

Iran / Iraq

Sensuous traffic paraded over the cobblestones.
The horse was skeletal when we rode him.
Right now I'm asleep with an Iranian princess in Aquamarine.
There's a hole in the map where the not me
is at knife point. You think I'm kidding:
my fascination with peeling her veils is absolutely unique—
shallow breathing, the sensations stampeding
and worthy of study. The whole history of men and women,
if we knew them as individuals . . . Then why am I shy
out-of-doors when my wallet's gratuitous,
a whisper in the theater? The streets are thin,
as in anonymous. Whose laundry hangs from the line
with a body on it, whose creeds—what, excite me?—
like smoked meats in the marketplace?
Then why not mention the milk factory
bombed to oblivion, the same oblivion
we draw from in the ashram?

My Country

I can't tell if it's a syndrome or a trajectory,
but now we can improve ourselves
by masquerading as something manufactured,
fractured, cut up. At cosmetic counters
we make ourselves over with a pencil
and a clear gel the color of the Pacific,
applying base to make our cheeks look rosier,
less interim. My country. Sure there are

national parks, splinter groups, sparks
at private parties. But once I possessed her
entirely. By possessed I mean the text is a fiction
whose purpose is to aggrandize the author,
and in a hospital outside Saigon,
my job was to shave pubic hair
until my patients became cherubic
with the sex parts of children.

But I sang to them to "get their minds off"
where incisions would be made.
Some had shrapnel in their thighs.
The delirious screamed at their sergeants.
Others lost their bearings orating long speeches.
Then came the scraping noise of helicopters,
which was like listening to Bruckner, hour

after hour of the same low hum: what was gradual
became invisible, what was sacred became scarred,
what was unsayable, what's the difference.

We don't want to follow our lives
from there, where policies are made,
where rhetoric drops over the antagonists.
Where we indulge in being driven to
and taking advantage, all the while feeling
"tossed aside," invisible, trailing behind the material
with a hole in it, the old gabardine suit, the ditch
it's buried in, the person we love inside it.

The Ex-Husband

I'm pure shrapnel, stored-up venom, a shred of a man,
a sliver, a desperate fighter cut on the lid, blindly
pummeling my opponent before going down.

Call it a compulsion, a fetish, an obsession, my face
in the window peering in, the face of a five-year-old begging
you to stare into that wallet full of need; at the same time

I feel the full force of me like a shove, a shove
inside me, a sinkhole or a ditch. Back there, the shutters
have been nailed down for the thunderstorm,

I overturn a wicker chair and a table looking for shelter
until the lightning strikes, until I see my face, as the storm
is sparking, alternating current: all self, no self, all self.

Scenario

The restricted clubs were sticky with ardor:
it was like being under an old car, changing the oil,
ratcheting free the muffler, serving them.

Of course they seemed content, full of self-expression,
complete with opinions like dress designs
from the fifties long after the blueprints lost their luster.

You have to imagine is no longer a viable strategy.
All the gaps, the lacunas, rifts between me and them
were singing in church and setting fire to the churches,

while the quilt on the club wall was a display of fabric
once loved, but now fashioned of borders and barricades.
Inside was a hovel, a burrow, a hole, the windows crushed glass

on the floor like rhinestones at the five-and-ten,
while she was a spiked collar under me in her strapless gown,
crossing the border, wearing a kerchief, affecting an accent

that would allay the guard's suspicion, the guard dogs
and the songs they growled, pale echoes of the calm
she must have known, must have known in the birthing room

the way I knew the hallway with the lights off
and the door locked, the whole crew of them knocking.
Outside: the traffic and trafficking, clamping a hand over your mouth.

Song

How sleepy the melody
of an afternoon, how slave-driven
those who dart in and out of it
on speeded-up film, till November's
out the door singing it's below zero
inside the butcher's freezer.
I turn to memory to eviscerate
the pasture: an erasure
with me beside it, beside the point,
lost in the hay grass. Perhaps
you've never been a shambles.
Then I envy you: you've never
been the one who roams the halls
asking if it's almost over, the night,
and how fatal is it? Maybe the surfaces
don't make you flinch, the dents
and catalysts: then you can report
the facts as if they were facts.
You can look the other way,
the luster of dew can't disperse you
with its intricacies and associations.
Then you're not here with me
inside a moment that means nothing
in and of itself, hugging the ground,
the slimy little worm cut
into segments. You've already turned
the other cheek to the infinite
softness of skin, the garbled birdsong
that sends out its thrush-like message.

I've Always Despised the Wetlands

I've always despised the wetlands
and their preserves, the gawky stork-like birds
squawking, standing endlessly on one leg
waiting for trout to leap onto their beaks—

the girth of them, the wingspan,
the smell half-sulfur, half-rotted pine
and something else smeared green
on the sewer pipe. I remember Traviata

on the tin can of a radio, tin cans
on the kitchen counter, a walk-up by the river,
a stench that made your eyes water
by the Dumpsters. Stab wounds on the boulevard.

You tried to break out by mangling
or burying your head in a book. Because patter
is terrible, being sunny, walking away
from a subject when shrieks cry out.

And sometimes you can't get a word in,
you don't want to forget, you want to straighten out
the sentence you've been given. I remember
a nest half-buried in a cedar. With an eyedropper

we fed the broken wren. A shoebox
would have been the right repository

for a voice on the edge of "terror," but only
a thin rope of words girded our neighborhood:

they were deficient little deficits, the signs
for Sanctuary and Refuge just beyond the fence,
where scattered birdcalls from a world
complete without us flourished, reminding me

how in snapshots Callas rose shining and waving
from the black limo, all ermine and pearls:
how she screened her lips when she threw fans kisses,
how wings are always attached to the singing.

Honeymoon in Florence

As they putty up their frescos,
as they scrape and file, the artisans of Florence
think this church in the Year of Our Lord,
think nature is nature, they think the olive
is an olive. They think the sentence
is an unshamed body part. The sentence
"buried in rubble" does not expect
sex trauma, stretch marks, chest scars,
the quick cut of collage, salutes
to the fractional, where I come from.

In the past we had blue cedars and country roads
with full-throated thrushes
laying down a sound track of pure sentiment.
From here you can see the olive groves of Tuscany,
where a statue can replace a worry,
and idiot savants hold out their arms
as if to receive an angel. What they rescued
was a fallen plaster crucifix
the year opening the door gave me vertigo,
and close friends were coughing away their cancers.

Something about me knocks keys off the vanity,
shouts from our hotel balcony: we're tired of trekking
through the mimetic woods to find some flower
to represent us, some psychic storm
to vanquish it. Underneath, in the shadow part,

the Tiepolos are swirling toward heaven
like a backwards flush of the toilet. Statues
die away at a very slow rate. Copperized monuments
are moldy with prattling, pecking sparrows.
Oh, I've been saved by love, but privately.

The Brightness

I'm no longer drawn
to the disaster parts of the story,
the dense shadows when the shade comes down

just before just before. I used to think,
What a dark spot I am. But there's something
about being tied up that likes to pout

and whimper, that likes to
do what she asks you. Hard to imagine,
the other side of the coin, if there were such a coin,

the July sky seamless, my eyes skylights—
enough sun to burn a hole in a leaf.
In the shower where the water's pinpricks,

under the waterfall you can't hear them
tell you what's good for you, what you want,
what it feels like. . . . If you thought feckless

meant joyless, if you thought the lyric speaker
rattled the slats of the dank little cattle car,
then we prayed to the same maker.

Material

Sometimes the whistling parts of the story
take over for the trembling parts, and while it's often steamy
to dig up *She said, How could you possibly,*
You wanted so much, maybe you know the place

where an idle space is less empty than serene,
a moment before lip service, before storm cellar
and should have, just before poets talk to the flowers
and confess their addictions, when some item

you can put in your hands is a benediction, a breastplate
for all those arrows that used to point your way,
and suddenly you can play the clarinet part of the concerto.
I'm stitching up the miscreant, paralyzed parts,

when whole weeks pass and you're still staring at the same page
on the same job, with the same wife, when the scabrous,
unjust shadows troll the neighborhood like cops looking for
whatever's hiding in the hallways that gets in their way.

Only a person with a lot of cash and a fathomless love
of God can say the material is degraded, shallow, an obstacle
to the fluffy clouds of somebody's heaven. I loved it
when the butcher entered the theater with his bloody smock.

Later someone named Ira digresses to the other neighborhood
and takes with him the scents of their stewing pots,

and OK, he can't stop scanning the body types, collecting them
for some future garbage can of an afternoon.

Now the dirge and the drill bit, the blame and the battering
can recede, now you can forgive, if you can't forgive
you can push past the gatekeepers, the men with white collars
who love stipulate and interim. Then I can look my mother's death in the face—

don't think I'd describe it for you—and the impossible passages
when I pursue the wrong woman for no reason,
the reason being I want to see her and be seen,
I can't turn the TV off with its Bosnias, Serbias, and Ruwandas

and all the other countries that are like spelling bees
and the gruel they're picking out of a bowl,
while flies buzz around them, stirs the entire afternoon.
There's nothing left to redeem of them,

so I apologize, I should be on my knees for this,
being so happy thinking of Caravaggio's
Judith and Holofernes, his head on a plate. I could describe
the slight of being cast aside, the crowd diving

after quarters that fell from her purse, Mexico City,
where my mother's always dreamed of, so if this is a dream,
I'm shaking her out of it. Get out of bed and finish the Marguerita,
you're not going to get the ending you want, the on-balance part,

the revelation that's a relief and a trophy. I'm being unfair,
sitting here with the window slightly open, the crackle
of thunder unfolding like static on a freshly laundered shirt,
waiting and not waiting for the next bolt. When the lights flicker,

when old selves are still dilating and deflecting,
when I'm chanting, staircase, body part, bombed-out cathedral,
if you want to know what stands behind the aura,
it's an angel, a human angel, sitting next to you

wiping your chin with a napkin.

I Forget Who Compared the Soul

to steam misting off a bowl of soup.
In the diner, she's craning her neck, conniving,
all she wants is to be recognized,
to be the waif who scrubs the floors of heaven
and pulls the pants down on a few granting angels.

Stripped down, how undone we look.
Who she slept with, where it got her, it consumes me.
What I hate about Dante is how he turns Envy
into a living breathing person who seduces you,
who you pursue until you're a belt he's unbuckling,

he's rattling all your inner furniture,
pressing your skull between his palms
until you feel the random, impersonal gusts
of the crevices that look down
on the way we craft a self out of sequence,

the way we become sleeves, the way
we sheathe our words so the way we're stapled
to each other is invisible. Next I'll be saying
there's a Nazi inside all of us, Evil's just a voice
inside us. Somewhere between the first jagged rip

of flesh and scar tissue that makes life bearable,
I see her brighten like a dial, the volume
turned all the way up, asking me if the soup's

ever been more than soup, dissolving into
spice and slice of carrot and potato, the slip of oil

that takes you to the wharf where you wanted to,
and I could make her teary and regretful,
except we're all wired together, so if one should spark . . .
What hacked tangles we are, so where else
could we turn but to the dense interior?

Illinois Poetry Series
Laurence Lieberman, Editor

Healing Song for the Inner Ear
Michael S. Harper (1984)

The Passion of the Right-Angled Man
T. R. Hummer (1984)

Dear John, Dear Coltrane
Michael S. Harper (1985)

Poems from the Sangamon
John Knoepfle (1985)

In It
Stephen Berg (1986)

The Ghosts of Who We Were
Phyllis Thompson (1986)

Moon in a Mason Jar
Robert Wrigley (1986)

Lower-Class Heresy
T. R. Hummer (1987)

Poems: New and Selected
Frederick Morgan (1987)

Furnace Harbor: A Rhapsody of the
North Country
Philip D. Church (1988)

Bad Girl, with Hawk
Nance Van Winckel (1988)

Blue Tango
Michael Van Walleghen (1989)

Eden
Dennis Schmitz (1989)

Waiting for Poppa at the Smithtown
Diner
Peter Serchuk (1990)

Great Blue
Brendan Galvin (1990)

What My Father Believed
Robert Wrigley (1991)

Something Grazes Our Hair
S. J. Marks (1991)

Walking the Blind Dog
G. E. Murray (1992)

The Sawdust War
Jim Barnes (1992)

The God of Indeterminacy
Sandra McPherson (1993)

Off-Season at the Edge of the World
Debora Greger (1994)

Counting the Black Angels
Len Roberts (1994)

Oblivion
Stephen Berg (1995)

To Us, All Flowers Are Roses
Lorna Goodison (1995)

Honorable Amendments
Michael S. Harper (1995)

Points of Departure
Miller Williams (1995)

Dance Script with Electric Ballerina
Alice Fulton (reissue, 1996)

To the Bone: New and Selected Poems
Sydney Lea (1996)

Floating on Solitude
Dave Smith (3-volume reissue, 1996)

Bruised Paradise
Kevin Stein (1996)

Walt Whitman Bathing
David Wagoner (1996)

Rough Cut
Thomas Swiss (1997)

Paris
Jim Barnes (1997)

The Ways We Touch
Miller Williams (1997)

The Rooster Mask
Henry Hart (1998)

The Trouble-Making Finch
Len Roberts (1998)

Grazing
Ira Sadoff (1998)

Turn Thanks
Lorna Goodison (1999)

Traveling Light:
Collected and New Poems
David Wagoner (1999)

Some Jazz a While:
Collected Poems
Miller Williams (1999)

The Iron City
John Bensko (2000)

Songlines in Michaeltree: New and
Collected Poems
Michael S. Harper (2000)

Pursuit of a Wound
Sydney Lea (2000)

The Pebble: Old and New Poems
Mairi MacInnes (2000)

Chance Ransom
Kevin Stein (2000)

House of Poured-Out Waters
Jane Mead (2001)

The Silent Singer: New and Selected
Poems
Len Roberts (2001)

The Salt Hour
J. P. White (2001)

Guide to the Blue Tongue
Virgil Suárez (2002)

The House of Song
David Wagoner (2002)

X =
Stephen Berg (2002)

Arts of a Cold Sun
G. E. Murray (2003)

Barter
Ira Sadoff (2003)

National Poetry Series

Eroding Witness
Nathaniel Mackey (1985)
Selected by Michael S. Harper

Palladium
Alice Fulton (1986)
Selected by Mark Strand

Cities in Motion
Sylvia Moss (1987)
Selected by Derek Walcott

The Hand of God and a Few
Bright Flowers
William Olsen (1988)
Selected by David Wagoner

The Great Bird of Love
Paul Zimmer (1989)
Selected by William Stafford

Stubborn
Roland Flint (1990)
Selected by Dave Smith

The Surface
Laura Mullen (1991)
Selected by C. K. Williams

The Dig
Lynn Emanuel (1992)
Selected by Gerald Stern

My Alexandria
Mark Doty (1993)
Selected by Philip Levine

The High Road to Taos
Martin Edmunds (1994)
Selected by Donald Hall

Theater of Animals
Samn Stockwell (1995)
Selected by Louise Glück

The Broken World
Marcus Cafagña (1996)
Selected by Yusef Komunyakaa

Nine Skies
A. V. Christie (1997)
Selected by Sandra McPherson

Lost Wax
Heather Ramsdell (1998)
Selected by James Tate

So Often the Pitcher Goes to Water until
It Breaks
Rigoberto González (1999)
Selected by Ai

Renunciation
Corey Marks (2000)
Selected by Philip Levine

Manderley
Rebecca Wolff (2001)
Selected by Robert Pinsky

Theory of Devolution
David Groff (2002)
Selected by Mark Doty

Other Poetry Volumes

Local Men and *Domains*
James Whitehead (1987)

Her Soul beneath the Bone: Women's
Poetry on Breast Cancer
Edited by Leatrice Lifshitz (1988)

Days from a Dream Almanac
Dennis Tedlock (1990)

Working Classics: Poems on Industrial Life
Edited by Peter Oresick and Nicholas Coles
(1990)

The University of Illinois Press
is a founding member of the
Association of American University Presses.

Composed in 10.5/13 Bembo
with Bembo display
by Jim Proefrock
at the University of Illinois Press
Designed by Paula Newcomb
Manufactured by Cushing-Malloy, Inc.

University of Illinois Press
1325 South Oak Street
Champaign, IL 61820-6903
www.press.uillinois.edu